A POCKET GUIDE TO
EGYPT

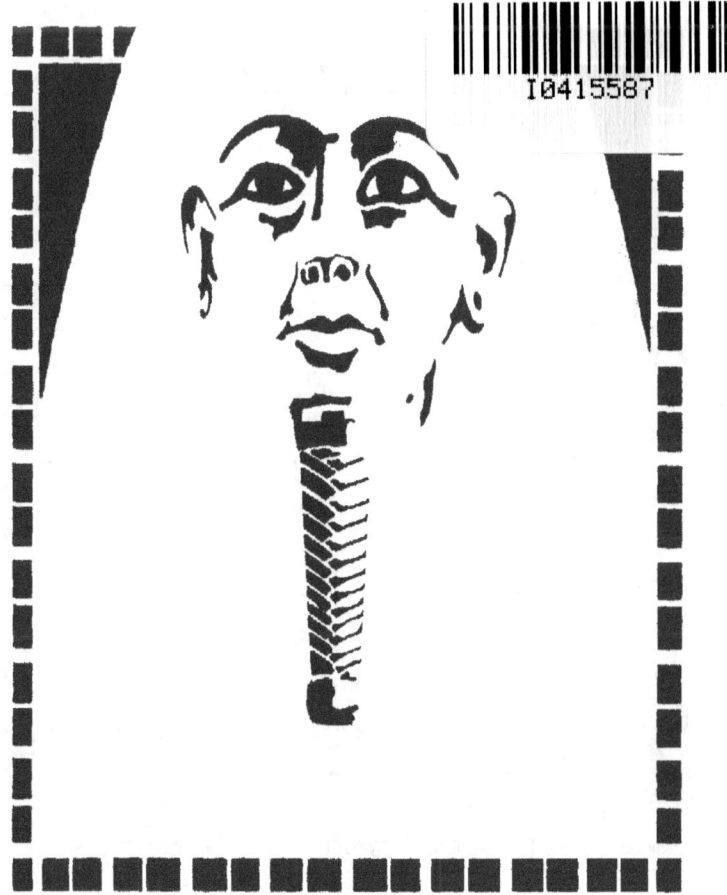

I0415587

American Forces Information Service • Washington, D.C. • 1988

DoD PG-10C*
DA Pam 360-402 (Rev. 1988)
NAVPERS 15420*
   Navy Stock No.0500 LP 175 4700
AFP 216-8 (Rev. 1988)
NAVMC 2722*

CONTENTS

*Replaces DoD PG-10B/DA Pam 360-402/NAVEDTRA 46510/AFP 216-8/NAVMC 2722,
which are obsolete.

A PROFILE OF EGYPT

Official Name: Arab Republic of Egypt

Capital: Cairo (over 11 million)

Other Cities: Alexandria (3 million), Giza (1.2 million), Shubra el Khema (393,000), Port Said (263,000)

Population: 50 million

Area: 1 million square kilometers (386,000 sq. mi.)

Literacy Rate: 44 percent

Per Capita Income: $686

Religions: Sunni Muslim, 90 percent; Coptic Christian

Languages: Arabic, English, French

Currency: Egyptian pound, divided into
100 piastres

Flag: Three horizontal stripes—
red, white and black (top to
bottom)—with an Egyptian
eagle in the center stripe

EGYPT'S ARMED FORCES

Egypt's armed forces are the largest in the region, totaling roughly 450,000 personnel divided into four services. The army is by far the largest—315,000—followed by air defense with 85,000, air force with 27,000 and navy with 32,000. Military equipment is primarily of Soviet origin, reflecting the long period of almost exclusively Soviet supply from the late 1950s until the 1973 war with Israel. Much of this equipment is now obsolete. Egypt's inventory also includes equipment from European sources—France, Italy, the United Kingdom—and China. Beginning in 1979, the United States entered into a military supply relationship with Egypt, resulting in major deliveries expected to continue throughout the 1980s. Egypt has a mutual defense treaty with Sudan and has provided military assistance and training to a number of African and Arab states, as it seeks to bolster stability and moderation in the region.

THE RELIGIONS

Islam

Islam, the religion of the great majority of your Egyptian hosts, is one of the world's fastest growing religions.

Today, an estimated 600 million men and women throughout the world are Muslims, and the religion is still spreading rapidly, especially on the African continent.

It is readily accepted by new members because the concepts are simple, there is no one between the believer and God, and through the (*Koran*), or Holy Book, the life of a Muslim is guided from birth through life to death and eternity.

Islam is the Arabic word for "submission."

A person who accepts Islam surrenders to the will of Allah (God).

This religion was founded by Muhammad, who was born of a merchant family in the trading city of Mecca in what is now Saudi Arabia in about 570 AD.

In his 40th year, after traveling with trading caravans throughout the Middle East, Muhammad had the first of a series of revelations from God through the angel Gabriel. During these trance-like states, Muhammad received over a period of time the contents of what is now the *Koran.*

Mecca at the time of Muhammad's young adulthood was the site of a number of pagan shrines located around a large black meteorite worshipped by the desert tribesmen. From the revelations, Muhammad soon started preaching that the pagan shrines must be closed and the city cleansed of its many different pagan idols. One God, Allah, was to take their place.

His preachings did not go well with the merchants of the city, who made their living selling goods to the worshippers at the many shrines. Muhammad was soon forced to flee Mecca.

His flight—*hegira*—took place in 622, a year that was later used as the first year when the Islamic calendar was started.

From Mecca he went first to Ta'if, where he preached his message of one God and was forced to flee again and then to Medina.

In Medina, Muhammad found a ready audience for his teachings. In addition to stating that there was only one God, Muhammad gave his followers simple rules to live by. If followed religiously, they would lead the believer to heaven.

As his following grew, so did his desire to return to Mecca, where he had first received the revelations. In 630, he returned at the head of an army, conquered Mecca and made it the holy city of Islam.

He died in 632, but his religion continued to grow. Within 100 years of his death, Islamic armies on their *jihad*—a holy war to spread the faith—had conquered an empire that soon was more extensive than that of Rome at its height.

Egypt was among the first countries to be invaded, and in a matter of two centuries the people there had abandoned both the Coptic language—in favor of Arabic—and Coptic Christianity to become Muslims.

All lands along the African coast of the Mediterranean were added to the Islamic Empire, as was much of what is now Spain, all of the Middle East and parts of India. Later, areas of what are now the USSR and China would have significant numbers of Muslims among their peoples.

But the death of Muhammad brought with it a religious split that remains in Islam to this day.

There were those Muslims who believed that the new leader of Islam should be selected from among the followers, as the leadership for a desert tribe was determined.

Other Muslims claimed that only a direct descendant of Muhammad could lead.

The first group, Sunni Muslims, is today the largest sect of Islam.

The second group, Shi'a Muslims, who believe that only descendants of Muhammad through his daughter, Fatima, and her husband, Ali, can be leaders, is concentrated mainly in Iran.

But, whatever the sect and wherever they are in the world, Muslims strive to follow the five pillars of Islam as laid down in the *Koran.*

These are:

• Recitation and belief in the Islamic creed that "There is no god but God, and Muhammad is His Prophet."

• The act of praying five times a day, facing Mecca, wherever a Muslim happens to be when the call to prayer is heard or it is time. The times for prayer are before sunrise, shortly after noon, in the late afternoon, immediately before sunset and just before retiring. Before each prayer session, the hands, face and feet must be washed. Mosques have special locations for this purpose, but in the desert, where water is rare, Muslims use sand to perform the symbolic act of washing.

• The giving of money to those poorer than themselves.

• Fasting between the hours of first light and sunset during the holy month of Ramadan, the ninth month in the Islamic calendar.

• Completion of a pilgrimage—*hajj*—to the holy city of Mecca by every Muslim who is financially and physically able to do so.

The Copts

The Egyptians were early converts to Christianity sometime in the first century after the death of Jesus.

They translated the Bible into Coptic, a language related to the language of the pharaohs. But in one of the early splits over the nature of God, the Coptic Christians broke with the rest of the church.

Coptic Christianity flourished in Egypt until 641, when the first waves of Islamic armies arrived, spreading their religion in a *jihad.*

Islam appealed immensely to the Egyptians, and within two centuries, the once-flourishing Coptic Christian church had been supplanted by Islam and the Coptic language by Arabic.

In Egypt, the Coptic Christian faith was kept alive in monasteries and convents, but never regained the popularity it once had.

An estimated 2 million Egyptians still practice Coptic Christianity, using a language that has been dead for 10 centuries in their rites.

A BIT OF HISTORY

Egypt is a land of ancient yesterdays, a thriving today and tomorrows of great promise.

It is a land of patient survivors. Its people have a continuous recorded history of more than 5,000 years—the longest in the Western world.

Ancient rulers—pharaohs—commanded tens of thousands of their citizens to build great memorials to their reigns and for their deaths. These memorials stand today, telling tales of riches beyond belief.

The burial site of one minor pharaoh, Tutankamun, yielded treasures when opened in 1922 that still astound all who view them in the Egyptian Museum of Cairo.

The tomb itself is located in the Valley of Kings in

Luxor, an ancient site that is visited by tens of thousands of tourists annually.

Another monument, the Pyramid of Cheops, one of three outside the capital city of Cairo, contains an estimated 6 million tons of limestone blocks. Each block is so tightly fitted against its neighbors that it is impossible to work a piece of paper in between.

Kings and conquerors came, ruled and died, but eternal Egypt and its people remained.

It was a united kingdom from about 3100 BC until Alexander the Great conquered it in 332 BC.

From then until the 20th century, it was under continuous foreign domination—by the Romans, the Persians, the Arabs (who introduced Islam and their language to the people), the Turks and the French.

The last period of foreign rule began in 1882, when the British occupied the nation to protect their interests in the Suez Canal, which opened in 1869.

The nation became a British protectorate in 1914, a monarchy in 1922 under King Fuad and a republic in June 1953.

Through the hard work of all Egyptians and the wisdom of the nation's leaders, Egypt today is acknowledged to be one of the most influential states in the Arab world.

Its population, educational system, industrial base and armed forces are the largest among the Arab nations.

You have an advantage in Egypt in that America and Americans are well-liked by the people.

The respect you show for the customs and culture of your host nation will add to our nation's image as a world leader.

If your mission permits the time, see some of the ancient and modern sights of Egypt.

Whatever you do, take the time to get to know your Egyptian hosts, both civilians and military. You'll find that they are friendly people, good hosts and our nation's friends.

THE EGYPTIANS

You will find the Egyptians a proud people, patient in their friendships with Americans.

They are proud of their past, which can be traced back some 5,000 years, one of the oldest continuous civilizations in the world.

And they are proud of their present-day progress and of their future as a leader in today's emerging Arab world.

They are a people unhurried in going about their everyday jobs and will not appreciate being rushed.

Patience is made necessary by the crowded conditions under which they live.

Some 98 percent of the nation's estimated 50 million citizens are crowded into less than 4 percent of the country's total area.

That is the fertile Nile valley. Centuries-old cities dot the river's banks, and two of the nation's largest cities—the capital of Cairo and the port of Alexandria—are on the delta the river has formed going into the Mediterranean.

Egypt has one of the highest population densities in the world. Just living from day to day takes patience.

And you will need patience also. The roads are narrow and packed with cars, people and carts. Transportation is hectic. But through all this, Egyptians are a happy-go-lucky people.

If a meeting is not started on time, it will be started later. If your Egyptian friend is to meet you at noon and comes two hours late, it is God's will. That's the Egyptian way of meeting the pressures of everyday life, and it should be your philosophy also when dealing with your hosts.

In your off-duty pursuits, relax and enjoy life as your Egyptian hosts do.

A WORD ABOUT TERRORISM

The likelihood of you or your family members being a victim of terrorism is smaller than well-publicized incidents would have you think. But the threat is real, more so in some places than others. Your local command in country should have the latest guidelines on terrorist activities affecting you and your family. With these guidelines and some common-sense approaches—the same ones you use to protect yourself against being a crime victim—you should feel free to enjoy the benefits of your overseas tour.

Enjoying your tour of duty and leisure time in your foreign county boils down to a few basic tips:

• Stay alert. Look around and notice what's going on. Follow your instincts if you feel uncomfortable about a situation.

• Keep a low profile. Avoid flashing money, wearing distinctively American clothing or otherwise bringing attention to yourself.

• Remain unpredictable. Vary your routine so it's difficult for someone to know when you'll be where and what route you'll follow to get there.

• Report any unusual activity that might be related to security to the appropriate authorities on your base or post.

GETTING AROUND

Many Egyptian cities may be reached by public transportation. An express train from Cairo to Alexandria takes 2½ hours and costs about $7 for a first-class seat, round trip. Day and night trips are available by train to Luxor and Aswan.

Pullman buses, with reserved seats and air-conditioning, serve Port Said, Ismailia, Suez and Alexandria.

Taxi rates are very cheap within cities, but you need some training to catch one. When you see a half-full taxi, wave your hand and shout the name of the place you wish to go. If the taxi is going that way, the driver will stop and pick you up.

Egypt Air, the only domestic air carrier, presently serves Aswan, Luxor, Hurghada, Abu Simbel and

Alexandria. Air Sinai, a branch of Egypt Air, provides scheduled service to the Sinai peninsula.

Driving in Egypt

Driving anywhere in Egypt is a challenge.

While there is every pressure on Egyptians to conform in social and religious life, hidden feelings seem to come out when they get behind the wheels of cars.

Roads and street signs with international icons are not frequent, and special indications are in Arabic only.

You will find that traffic lights mean little or nothing to the average driver or pedestrian. Drive defensively every moment.

YOU AND THE LAW

Since the United States has no Status of Forces Agreement with Egypt, you may be subject to applicable Egyptian laws while a guest in that country.

Driving

Egyptian drivers licenses are required. You may apply for one on arrival. All car owners must carry third-party liability insurance according to Egyptian law and policy. Although other coverage is not legally mandatory, it is practical. Accidents are frequent.

If you are involved in an accident, ask the local police officer to contact your unit, if possible, or the nearest American installation or the U.S. Embassy.

Firearms

Only the following non-automatic firearms and ammunition may be brought into Egypt: one small-bore rifle, one shotgun and 500 rounds of ammunition for each weapon. They may be shipped, but not mailed, to your installation, provided they are consigned to U.S. personnel for personal use and not for resale.

Send notification of your intent to import firearms as soon as possible, because customs clearance takes two or three months. You must provide four passport photos and the firearms model and serial numbers and whether single or double barrel. Gun permits must be reissued annually.

Before departing Egypt, you must obtain permission to export the firearms from your local police precinct.

GETTING ALONG

The Arab world is a man's world.

This is true even in Egypt, where you will see women working in either traditional or modern dress in every walk of life.

There is still a very protective feeling among the men when it comes to the women of their family.

Contacts with Egyptian women must be confined to whatever business is at hand. To go any further would be to invite trouble.

Remember that it is forbidden to aggressively approach a female. In addition, a male is not allowed to visit a female at her home if she is there alone. Males can visit only if another man such as a father, husband or brother is present.

Photographing Egyptians is permitted as long as you don't focus on the person without having first asked permission. A good rule to follow while in Egypt: Do not attempt to photograph women, whether you see them in the streets of a modern city or on country lanes. But if you just have to have the picture, ask first, but don't be aggressive. You may also find that many of the men resent being photographed.

If the answer is "no," don't take the photograph!

You should also remember that public law and the *Koran* prohibit kissing and hugging in public places and that short pants or short skirts that expose the thighs are culturally unacceptable. Showing a bare chest and back (no shirt) in public, except on the beach, is also unacceptable.

While Americans are considered as friends by the majority of Egyptians, you must be sensitive to their customs.

You will find Egyptian men open and friendly to Americans. Their friendliness does not open the way for the more intimate questions that Americans ask one another. You should never ask a man why he believes in the "evil eye" and wears a charm against its effects or about female members of his family.

If you are entertained by an Egyptian friend, it will be at a coffee house or in a restaurant.

There you will discover that Egyptians are an emotional and expressive people. They love physical contact with those about them and may hold your hand or arm while talking to you. When you first enter a room where there are Egyptians, walk around and gently shake the hands of everyone. It's expected and is a good way to make friends. Do the same when you leave a room.

In a coffee house, what may sound like a hot argument to you will be only a polite discussion to your Egyptian friends. Ideas are expressed at full voice, everyone talks, and few listen. It can be fun, so sit back and relax.

Whatever you do, however, do not get involved in discussions about politics, religion, the Middle East situation or any other controversial subject.

This is an important point, since to many of your Egyptian friends you will represent America. Keep your comments confined to complimentary remarks about the country and its people.

Compliments are a way of life in Egypt and else-where in the Arab world. You will hear compliments about the United States, prayers for your health and expressions of "long life."

Follow suit. Compliment your Egyptian friend on a job well done, on the history and beauty of his country and on your hopes for his country's future.

When you enter an office on business or meet an Egyptian friend on the street, you will be invited to share in something to drink. It could be tea, coffee or a soft drink. To refuse is considered rude in most situations; however, if the offer is from a friend and you don't wish to eat or drink, you don't have to accept. A simple "No, thank you" is acceptable. A friend will not be offended. Otherwise, accept the offer, enjoy the drink and take time to pass a few minutes in conversation before starting to discuss any business you have in mind.

In the same manner, if Egyptians visit your office or work area, offer them something to drink.

Since the Islamic religion forbids the use of intoxicants, do not offer alcohol to Egyptian guests. Alcoholic beverages are on sale in Egypt because of the large numbers of tourists who visit the country each year. But unless you know your guest's taste, do not offer alcoholic beverages at cafes or parties.

When offering anything—a beverage, food, cigarettes—to an Arab and while you are eating, always use your right hand. Do this even though you may be left-handed. To offer something to an Arab with the left hand is an insult, since the left hand in the Arab world is used only for the body's private functions.

Also, when in the company of Egyptians or other Arabs, be careful in crossing your legs and showing the sole of your shoe or foot. This traditionally has been considered to be in bad taste. But this is changing in modern Egypt. Many Egyptians no longer consider crossing the legs and showing the soles of shoes offensive.

On the streets and elsewhere, show every respect for the religious beliefs of your hosts. As Muslims, they answer the call to prayer five times a day and will stop in the street or on sidewalks to face toward Mecca, kneel and offer their prayers. If this happens, stand quietly to one side until the prayers are over.

Mosques in Egypt are open to all, including non-Muslims, as long as shoes are removed. This practice has to do with the fact that Muslims touch their foreheads to the ground during prayer. The removal of shoes also helps to maintain a quiet atmosphere within the mosque. If you visit a mosque, it is best to be escorted by an Egyptian friend who can explain the various areas to you. Taking photographs is permitted in some of the more famous and historic mosques; however, it would probably be an annoyance to worshippers in many local mosques and should not be done.

If you are in Egypt during the holy month of Ramadan, respect the Muslims' requirements to fast. Do not offer food, beverages or cigarettes during the hours of fasting (from first light to sunset) or eat or smoke in front of a Muslim during those hours. Tempers can be short at this time of the year, and extra consideration is needed.

SIZING UP

The metric system of measuring is used in most of the world's countries; the United States is an exception to this rule.

It is a simple system and one that you will get used to in a matter of weeks. To aid you, here are some approximate comparisons.

Length-Distance

1 inch = 2.54 centimeters

1 centimeter = 0.3937 inches

1 foot = 30.48 centimeters

1 meter = 39.37 inches

1 yard = 91.44 centimeters

1 meter = 1.09 yards

1 mile = 1.61 kilometers

1 kilometer = 0.621 mile

Weight

1 gram	= 0.035 ounces
10 grams	= 0.35 ounces
100 grams	= 3.52 ounces (approx. ¼ lb.)
500 grams (1/2K)	= 17.52 ounces (approx. 1 lb.) + 2 ounces
1,000 grams (1 K)	= 35.27 ounces (approx. 2 lbs. + 3 ounces)

For an approximate quick conversion of pounds into kilos, divide pounds by 2.2. Example: 6 lbs, 6 ozs divided by 2.2 = 2.898 kilos.

For an approximate quick conversion of kilos into pounds, multiply kilos by 2.2. Example: 3 kilos, 500 grams x 2.2 = 7 lbs, 11 ozs; 3 kilos, 50 grams (3.050) x 2.2 = 6 lbs, 11 ozs.

Pound/Kilo Comparisons

1 pound	= .453 Kilograms
2 pounds	= .9072 Kilograms
3 pounds	= 1.360 Kilograms
4 pounds	= 1.814 Kilograms
5 pounds	= 2.268 Kilograms
10 pounds	= 4.536 Kilograms

Liquids

1 liter	= 1.05 quarts
1 quart	= .946 liters
1 U.S. gallon	= 3.785 liters

Liter/Gallon Comparisons

5 liters	= 1.32 gallons
10 liters	= 2.64 gallons
15 liters	= 3.98 gallons
20 liters	= 5.28 gallons

25 liters	= 6.61 gallons
30 liters	= 7.93 gallons
35 liters	= 9.25 gallons

Speed Comparisons

6.2 MPH = 10 KPH	40.3 MPH = 65 KPH
9.3 MPH = 15 KPH	43.4 MPH = 70 KPH
12.4 MPH = 20 KPH	46.6 MPH = 75 KPH
15.5 MPH = 25 KPH	49.7 MPH = 80 KPH
18.6 MPH = 30 KPH	52.8 MPH = 85 KPH
21.7 MPH = 35 KPH	55.9 MPH = 90 KPH
24.8 MPH = 40 KPH	59 MPH = 95 KPH
27.9 MPH = 45 KPH	62.1 MPH = 100 KPH
31 MPH = 50 KPH	65.2 MPH = 105 KPH
34.1 MPH = 55 KPH	68.3 MPH = 110 KPH
37.2 MPH = 60 KPH	71.6 MPH = 115 KPH
	74.6 MPH = 120 KPH

Metric Conversion Factors

You will soon get used to metric measures. Here are some approximate conversion methods that will help you get a start.

Length

When you know—	Multiply by—	To Find—
inches	2.5	centimeters
centimeters	0.4	inches
feet	30	centimeters
meters	3.3	feet

When you know—	Multiply by—	To Find—
yards	0.9	meters
meters	1.1	yards
miles	1.6	kilometers
kilometers	0.6	miles

Area

When you know—	Multiply by—	To Find—
square inches	6.5	square centimeters
square centimeters	0.16	square inches
square feet	0.09	square meters
square yards	0.8	square meters
square meters	1.2	square yards
square miles	2.6	square kilometers
square kilometers	0.4	square miles

Mass

When you know—	Multiply by—	To Find—
ounces	28	grams
grams	0.035	ounces
pounds	0.45	kilograms
kilograms	2.2	pounds

Volume

When you know—	Multiply by—	To Find—
teaspoons	5	milliliters
milliliters	0.2	teaspoons
tablespoons	15	milliliters
milliliters	0.7	tablespoons
fluid ounces	30	milliliters
milliliters	0.03	fluid ounces
cups	0.24	liters
liters	4.2	cups
pints	0.47	liters
liters	2.1	pints
quarts	0.95	liters
liters	1.06	quarts
gallons	3.8	liters
liters	0.26	gallons

Clothing Sizes Comparisons

MEN

Suits, Overcoats, Sweaters

United States								
34	35	36	37	38	39	40	41	42
Great Britain*								
34	35	36	37	38	39	40	41	42
European 44	46	48	49½	51	52½	54	55½	57

Shirts

United States	14	14½	15	15½	16	16½	17	17½
Great Britain*	14	14½	15	15½	16	16½	17	17½
European	36	37	38	39	41	42	43	44

Socks

United States	9½	10	10½	11	11½
Great Britain*	9½	10	10½	11	11½
European	38/39	39/40	40/41	41/42	42/43

Shoes

United States	7	8	9	10	11	12	13
Great Britain*	6	7	8	9	10	11	12
European	39½	41	42	43	44½	46	47

WOMEN

Dresses, Coats, Suits

United States	8	10	12	14	16	18	20
Great Britain*	30	32	33	35	36	38	39
European	36	38	40	42	44	46	48

Blouses, Sweaters

United States	10	12	14	16	18	20	22	24
	(30)	(32)	(34)	(36)	(38)	(40)	(42)	(44)
Great Britain*	32	34	36	38	40	42	44	46
European	38	40	42	44	46	48	50	52

Stockings

United States	8	8½	9	9½	10	10½	11
Great Britain*	8	8½	9	9½	10	10½	11
European	0	1	2	3	4	5	6

Shoes

United States	4	4½	5	5½	6	6½	7	7½	8
Great Britain*	2½	3	3½	4	4½	5	5½	6	6½
European	35	35½	36	36½	37	37½	38	38½	39

Gloves:

Glove sizes are standard in the United States, Great Britain and Europe.

*Note: Since Great Britain joined the Common Market, both British and European sizes may be found in most articles of clothing. If in doubt, try the article on first.

LANGUAGE GUIDE

Arabic is a very expressive language, one filled with flowery compliments, prayers and good wishes. Like most people, Arabs consider their language to be one of the most beautiful in the world. Learn a few of the following words and phrases. Your pronunciation may not be the best, but it will please your Egyptian hosts if you try.

Greetings and General Phrases

English	Approximate Arabic Pronunciation
Please	Mm fadlak
Thank you	Shukran
Welcome	Ahlan wa sahlan

Yes	Na'am
No	La
Don't mention it	'Afwan
Sorry; Excuse me	Mut'assif
How are you?	Kaif halak
Well	Tayyib
Good morning	Sabah al-khair
Good morning (reply)	Sabah an-nur
Good evening	Masa' al-khair
Goodbye	Fi aman illah
Goodbye (reply)	Ma'a as-salama
This	Hadha
That	Dhalika
How much?	Qiddash
Where is...?	Fain...?
the market	suq
police station	markiz il-bolis
On your left	'Ala shimaluk
On your right	'Ala yaminuk
Straight ahead	Dogri
Go!	Imshi!
When?	Emta?
Come!	Ta'ala!
Stop!	Qif!

Do you speak English?	Tatakallam inglizi?
Money	Flous
Gasoline	Benzin
Tea	Shahi
Coffee	Qahwa
Sugar	Sukkar

Numbers

One	Wahad	Nine	Tis'a
Two	Itnin	Ten	'Ashara
Three	Thalatha	Fifteen	Khamsatash
Four	Arb'a	Twenty	'Ashrin
Five	Khamsa	Fifty	Khamsin
Six	Sitta	One Hundred	Mia
Seven	Sab'a	One Thousand	Alf
Eight	Tamanya		

Days

Sunday	Yaum al-ahad
Monday	Yaum al'itnin
Tuesday	Yaum ath-thalath
Wednesday	Yaum al-arba
Thursday	Yaum al-khamis
Friday	Yaum al-jum'a
Saturday	Yaum as-sabt

SITES TO SEE

In Egypt, you have an opportunity to visit some of the outstanding sites in world history. Without leaving metropolitan Cairo, you can see the walls of the citadel that Saladin built to withstand the Crusaders; medieval Islamic houses with harem windows and restful, private gardens; and mausoleums, mosques and palaces.

Many fascinating archeological sites are within a day's drive of Cairo: the pyramids and the tombs of Giza, Saqqara, Memphis, Meidum and Hawarra. Two nearby villages, Harrania and Kerdassa, are known for their fabric and weaving.

Traditional crafts are taught in craft centers in Cairo, supported by the Ministry of Culture. You can wander down a street of tentmakers and saddle-makers, see glass blowers and a ceramist.

Cairo may be seen at your leisure, armed with a guidebook, a map and a few words of Arabic, or you can join a tour arranged by the American University in Cairo.

The Mediterranean beaches west of Alexandria are beautiful. Several resort hotels are available there, plus a guest house and apartments that may be rented.

Hurghada and the Red Sea may be visited by Egypt Air. Travel agents can arrange other excursions, such as a boat trip down the Nile from Luxor to Cairo.

YOU AND THE DESERT

Working and living in the desert environment of Egypt is not the same as working on a hot day in the United States.

Egypt is a true desert. Extremely high temperatures during the daytime, coupled with extremely low humidity, can quickly lead to heat exhaustion or heat stroke.

Because of these dangers, it is necessary to increase liquid intake dramatically.

You should drink at least two or three quarts of water a day, more if you still feel like it. And take a supply of sunscreen lotion and lip balm to prevent sunburn and drying out.

Eye and respiratory problems can also occur in desert operations.

Sunglasses are necessary during all daylight hours. In extreme cases, eye injuries have occurred from the glare of the sunlight on the sand or a body of water such as the Mediterranean or the Red Sea. Eye drops may be necessary to flush out the sand that is constantly in the air.

Airborne sand also can cause breathing and respiratory problems.

Take a lesson from your Egyptian friends—keep your body covered while working in the sun, even though it may be uncomfortable. This is especially true for the head. You should wear head covering at all times during daylight hours.

FOOD

Cairo has abundant fresh fruits and vegetables, meats and poultry and many imported food items.

Lamb, beef and veal can be purchased in butcher shops only on Thursday, Friday and Saturday. Chicken, goose, duck, turkey and pigeon are available every day. For religious reasons, pork is sold only in special shops. Excellent varieties of fish are available in the markets.

Fruits and vegetables are seasonal and usually inexpensive. Local vegetables include potatoes, onions, garlic, lettuce, tomatoes, cucumbers, squash, celery, green beans, beets, carrots, green and red cabbage, spinach, okra, radishes, turnips, eggplant, parsley, dill and mint. Some local fruits are bananas, apples, grapefruit, lemons, tangerines, oranges, mangoes, melons, dates, figs, papayas, gooseberries, strawberries, pears, coconuts, persimmon, pomegranates and grapes.

Cairo has reasonably good restaurants, including cruising restaurants featuring Egyptian, European and Middle Eastern menus. Restaurants usually open at 8 p.m. Reservations are required.

TIME AND DATE

Time

There is a seven-hour difference in time between New York City on Eastern Standard Time and Cairo. When it is noon in New York City, it is 7 p.m. in Cairo.

Date

In Egypt you will see three dates on newspapers and documents.

One date will show the day, month and year of the Gregorian calendar, one you are already familiar with.

The second date will be followed by the letters "AH," *Anno Hegirae.*

This date relates to the Islamic calendar that was

started in the seventh century. The first year of that calendar was the year of Muhammad's flight—hegira—from Mecca to Ta'if to Medina in 622 A.D.

A year in this calendar has 354 days in 12 lunar months, a month being the time between two new moons. Since that period is approximately $29\frac{1}{2}$ days, the calendar was adjusted into months of alternating 29 and 30 days. Leap year days are added every five years to further adjust the calendar.

Since the Islamic calendar is based on the lunar cycle, the months of the year have no fixed relation to the seasons, but instead make a complete circuit through the seasons every 33 Gregorian years.

The first month of the Islamic year is *Muharram*, followed by *Safar, Rabi al Awwal, Rabi ath Thani, Jumada al Ula, Jumada al Akhirah, Rajab, Shaban, Ramadan*—the month of fasting, *Shawwal, Dhu Al Qadah*, and *Dhu Al Hijjah*, the month in which the journey should be made to Mecca.

The third date, the Coptic month and date, is printed in Arabic-language newspapers since it is used by farmers to plant and sow their crops.

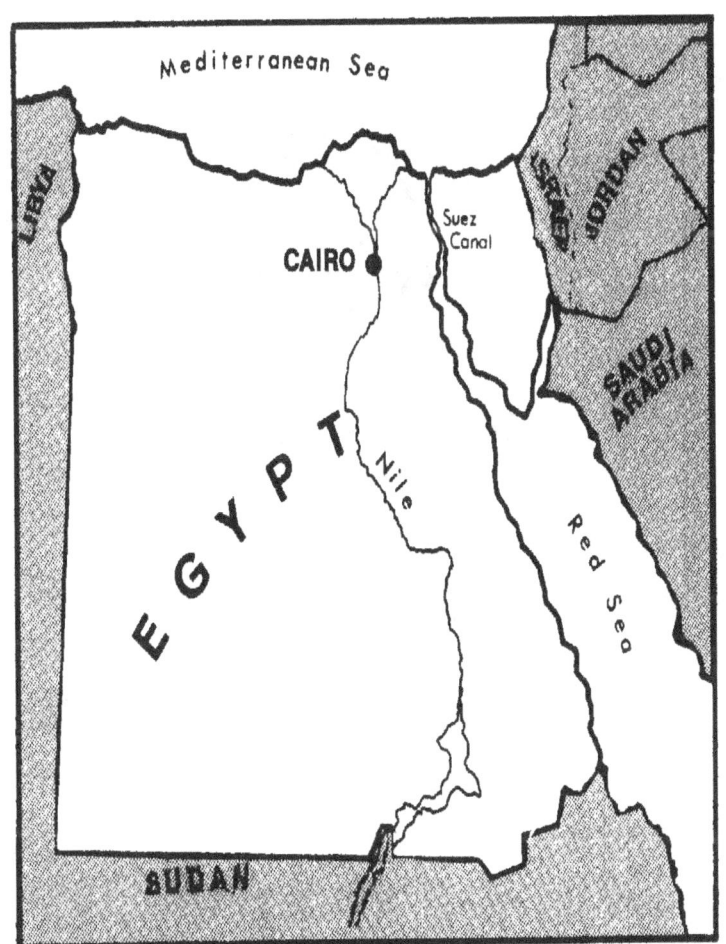

The Secretary of Defense
Washington, D.C.
December 1988

A POCKET GUIDE TO EGYPT (DoD PG-10C). This
official Department of Defense publication is for the use of
personnel in the military services.